CHILDREN'S BIBLE STORIES

From the Old Testament

retold by
Ruth Hannon

Illustrated by Joe Giordano

g|b **Golden Press · New York**

Western Publishing Company, Inc.
Racine, Wisconsin

CONTENTS

GOD MAKES THE WORLD

Once, very long ago,
there was no land or sea.
There were no people or animals or plants.
There were no stars or even clouds.
God lived alone in the darkness.
There was no light anywhere until God said,
"Let there be light!"
At once light came into the darkness.
Then God made the sky, water and land.
He made trees, flowers and plants of all kinds.
He made the sun to light the day.
He made the moon to light the night.
God filled the seas with fish and whales
and dolphins and other living things.
He put birds into the trees.
He made animals and creeping things.
And he gave them the earth for a home.
God had made the world.
He had filled it with beautiful things.
But still there were no men or women,
no boys or girls in God's lovely new world.

GENESIS 1

ADAM AND EVE

The Lord God said,
"I shall make man to rule the earth."
He picked up some dust from the ground.
He shaped it to look like a man.

The Lord God breathed into that dust.
At once it became alive.
It was Adam, the first man.

Then the Lord God made a garden in Eden.
He said to Adam, "This will be your home."

Trees and plants grew in the garden.
Birds sang in the trees.
Animals played in the grass.
Adam gave a name to every animal.

But no other people lived in the garden.
And Adam was very lonely.

Then the Lord God made a woman.
He called her Eve.
And Adam and Eve were happy in Eden.

It took God six days to make the world.
In those six days He made Adam and Eve, too.
But on the seventh day God rested from his work.

GENESIS 2

8

NOAH'S ARK

Many years passed.
A great many people now lived on the earth.
But the Lord saw only one good person.
This was a man named Noah.

The Lord said to Noah,
"Very soon I shall send heavy rains.
They will wash the wicked from the earth.
But I shall save you and your family."

And the Lord told Noah,
"Build an ark of many rooms.
Take into it your wife and your sons.
And take into it a male and a female
of every kind of animal."

Noah and his three sons set to work.
They built an ark, as the Lord had said.
Into it marched Noah's family
and two of every kind of animal.

Then the rain began to fall.
It fell for forty days and forty nights.
Before long, water covered the earth.
It covered every hill and mountain.
But the ark floated safely on the waves.

Soon no living thing was left on the earth.
Only those inside the ark were still alive.

After a time, the skies cleared.
And Noah's ark came to rest on a mountain.
But water still covered the earth.
    Noah waited a few weeks.
Then he let a dove fly from a window.
But she never went back to the ark.
    "The earth must be dry," said Noah.
"The dove has found a place to rest."
    Then Noah and his family marched
out of the ark with all the animals.
And Noah built a place to worship.
There he praised the Lord and thanked him.

GENESIS 6-8

ABRAM IN THE LAND OF CANAAN

A man named Abram lived in Haran.
But the Lord said to him, "Leave this place.
Go to the land I shall show you."

At once Abram set out with his wife Sarai.
Lot, his brother's son, went along, too.
They took their servants and their sheep and cattle.

Day after day they marched across hot sands.
They found very little water in that desert.
There was not much grass for their animals, either.

At last Abram and Lot came to a well.
It was filled with good, cool water.
Thick grass grew around it.

There Abram and Lot put up their tents.
The servants led the animals out to the grass.

But Lot's servants said to Abram's,
"Take your animals away.
This grass will not feed all our animals.
There is not enough of it."
The men began to fight with one another.

Abram said to Lot,
"There is only one way to stop this fighting.
You and I must part.
Do you want to go to the right?
Then I shall go to the left."

12

Lot took his animals to the right.
He stopped at grassy fields near a river.
    Abram went up into the mountains.
He found a dry place with not much grass.
    There the Lord came to him and said,
"Abram, lift up your eyes.
Look to the north and to the south.
Look to the east and to the west.
I shall give you all the land you see.
It is the land of Canaan.
It will belong to you
and to your children forever."
    Abram said,
"But Sarai and I have no children, Lord."
    Then the Lord said,
"From now on your name will be Abraham.
And your wife Sarai will be called Sarah.
Next year you and Sarah will have a son.
You must call him Isaac."
    Next year Sarah and Abraham had a son.
They called him Isaac, as the Lord had said.

GENESIS 12, 13, 15, 17, 21

THE SONS OF ISAAC

Isaac and his wife, Rebekah, had two sons.
Esau, the older, liked to hunt.
But Jacob, the younger brother, was quiet.
He liked to sit at home in his tent.

In those days a father left most
of his land and animals to his older son.
And so Esau would get most of Isaac's goods.

One morning Esau went out to hunt.
On his way home he smelled something good.
"Jacob is making vegetable soup," he thought.
And he went into his brother's tent.

"Jacob," said Esau, "I am hungry.
Please give me some of your soup."

"You may have some," said Jacob.
"But first you must give me your right
to father's land and animals."

Esau said, "I am very hungry.
I think I shall die if I do not eat.
Then how could I use father's goods?
I give you my right to all he owns."

Then Jacob gave Esau the soup.
In return, Esau gave Jacob the right
to their father's land and animals.

GENESIS 25

14

A LADDER TO HEAVEN

One day Jacob set out on a long trip.
When night came he was very tired.

"I shall sleep on the ground," he said.
Under his head he put a stone.
Soon he was fast asleep and dreaming.

In his dream he saw a ladder.
It reached all the way to heaven.
Some angels were going up the ladder.
Others were coming down.

The Lord stood above the ladder.
And He said to Jacob,
"I am the God of Abraham and of Isaac.
I shall give this land to you and your children.
You will go to other lands.
But you will always come back to this place."

Jacob woke up.
He said, "I know the Lord is here.
This is the house of God.
It is the gate of heaven."

He took the stone under his head
and he poured oil upon it.

He called that place Bethel,
meaning "God's House."

GENESIS 28

YOUNG JOSEPH

Jacob had many sons.
But the one he loved best was Joseph.

Now Jacob gave Joseph a fine coat.
It had long sleeves and colored stripes.

The angry, jealous brothers said,
"Father does not give fine coats to us."
And they turned away from Joseph.

Then the brothers set out with their sheep.
They took them far away to find grass and water.
But Joseph stayed home with his father.

The brothers were gone for many weeks.

One day Jacob said to Joseph,
"Go and see what your brothers are doing."

The brothers saw Joseph coming.
"Here comes father's favorite son," they said.
"Let's get rid of him."

They pulled off Joseph's coat,
and they threw him into a pit.

Far away they saw men coming.
One brother said,
"Let us sell Joseph to these fellows."
The men took Joseph to Egypt.
Then the brothers said to their father,
"Wild animals have eaten Joseph."
Jacob believed them and he began to cry.
He thought the son he loved was dead.

GENESIS 37

17

JOSEPH IN PRISON

In Egypt Joseph was sold to Potiphar.
This man was an officer in the army of Egypt.
He served under the Pharaoh, Egypt's king.

Joseph worked hard as a slave for Potiphar.
But Potiphar's wife told lies about the Hebrew.
And he was put into prison.

Joseph made friends with a man in prison.
This man had been the Pharaoh's butler.
Soon he and Joseph became good friends.

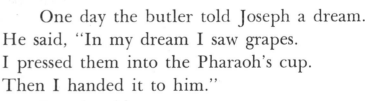

One day the butler told Joseph a dream.
He said, "In my dream I saw grapes.
I pressed them into the Pharaoh's cup.
Then I handed it to him."

Joseph said,
"This means you will be freed in three days.
Again you will be the Pharaoh's butler.
Again you will give him wine in a cup."

Three days later the butler was set free.
He went back to work in the Pharaoh's palace.

But still Joseph was in prison.
It seemed that he would never be free.

GENESIS 39, 40

JOSEPH AT THE PHARAOH'S COURT

The Pharaoh of Egypt had a dream.
Not one person could tell him what it meant.
But his butler said, "Send for Joseph."

Joseph was soon brought from the prison.
And the Pharaoh said to him,
"In a dream I saw seven fat cows.
But seven thin cows ate them.
Then I saw seven good ears of corn.
But seven thin ears ate the good ones."

Joseph said, "I know what this means.
Egypt will have seven good years.
Then Egypt will have seven bad years.
In those years very little grain will grow."

The Pharaoh asked, "What shall I do?"
Joseph said, "Set a wise man over Egypt.
In the good years he can store away grain."
The Pharaoh said, "Joseph, you are wise.
You are the man I shall set over Egypt."
For seven years Joseph stored away grain.
Then came seven years when no grain grew.
But all the people had food in those bad years.
For Joseph gave them grain he had stored away.
And not one person went hungry.

GENESIS 41

19

JOSEPH'S BROTHERS

Joseph's father and brothers lived in Canaan.
But they had no grain to eat.
And their children were crying for food.

Jacob said to his sons,
"Go to Egypt and buy grain for bread."

In Egypt the brothers went to the market.
Joseph was there, giving orders to his men.
He saw his brothers and he knew them.
But not one of them knew him.

The brothers bowed to Joseph and said,
"Sir, we have come to buy grain."

Joseph sold them all they wanted.
Then he held out his arms to them.
"Don't you know me?" he asked.
"I am Joseph your brother."

He was not angry with his brothers.
He loved every one of them.

"Bring my father to Egypt," he said.
"I want all of you to live here.
You may have the best land in the country.
You may have the land of Goshen."

Jacob and his sons went to Egypt to live.
There they found grass and water for their animals.
And they and their children were very happy.

GENESIS 42-46

20

MOSES, THE HEBREW BABY

A cruel Pharaoh sat on the throne in Egypt.
He said, "There are too many Hebrews in Egypt.
Throw every Hebrew boy baby into the river."

Soon after that, a Hebrew boy baby was born.
His mother hid him for a while.
Then she put him into a basket.
She took it to the river's edge.
And there she set the basket among the reeds.

The baby's sister, Miriam, hid nearby.
Soon an Egyptian princess came down to the river.
She saw the basket among the reeds.
"Bring it to me," she told her servant.

The princess took the cover from the basket.
She smiled at the tiny baby lying there.
"It is one of the Hebrews' children," she cried.

Then Miriam came out from hiding.
"I know a Hebrew woman," she told the princess.
"She will take care of the baby, I am sure."

"Bring her to me," said the princess.

Miriam's mother took her boy baby home.
She loved him and cared for him.
After a year she took him back to the princess.

The princess said, "This child will be my son.
I shall call him Moses."

EXODUS 1, 2

MOSES AND THE BURNING BUSH

Moses grew to be a fine young man.
He had been raised like an Egyptian.
But he knew he was a Hebrew.
He knew, too, that other Hebrews were slaves.
They had to do the hardest work in Egypt.

Once Moses saw an Egyptian beating a Hebrew.
Moses hit the Egyptian and the man died.

Someone told the story to the Pharaoh.
"Moses will die for this!" cried the Pharaoh.

But the Hebrew ran away to another country.
In that strange land he worked as a shepherd.

One day Moses led his sheep to Mount Horeb.
There he saw a most wonderful thing.
Fire was coming from a bush.
But the bush was not being burned.

A voice called from the bush, "Moses! Moses!
I am the God of Abraham and Isaac.
I want you to lead my people out of Egypt.
Take your brother Aaron and go to the Pharaoh.
Tell him to let the Hebrews go."

EXODUS 2-4

23

MOSES, THE LEADER

Moses set out to obey the Lord.
First he and his brother Aaron went to Egypt.
Moses told the Hebrew slaves, "God has heard you.
He wants me to lead you out of Egypt."
The Hebrews cried, "God has remembered his people."
Moses and Aaron then visited the Pharaoh.
"Hear what the Lord tells you," they said.
"You must let the Hebrews go out of Egypt."
"No," said the Pharaoh. "They will never go."
And he made things even harder for them.
He gave an order to the Egyptian leaders,
"Make the Hebrew slaves work harder."
Moses heard about this and he cried to the Lord,
"See what the Pharaoh is doing to your people?
He is killing them with hard work."
And the Lord said, "Go back to the Pharaoh.
He will ask you for a sign.
Then Aaron must throw down his rod."
They did as the Lord had said.
Aaron threw down his rod at the Pharaoh's feet.
It turned into a snake.
Then Pharaoh's wise men threw down their rods.
They turned into snakes, too.
But Aaron's rod ate up all the others.
Still the Pharaoh would not let the Hebrews go.

And the Lord said to Moses,
"Let Aaron hold his rod over the river Nile."
Aaron did this and the water turned red.
But the Pharaoh would not let the Hebrews go.
      Then the Lord covered the land with frogs.
But the Pharaoh would not let the Hebrews go.
      The Lord sent more trouble to the Egyptians.
Hail fell and killed the trees.
Locusts ate the plants.
The land was dark as night for three days.
But the Pharaoh would not let the Hebrews go.
      Then the Lord said to Moses,
"Tell the people to get ready to go out of Egypt.
One night soon I will pass over the land.
And I shall change the heart of the Pharaoh.
That night will be the Passover of the Lord."
      The Hebrews got ready, as the Lord had said.
And the night of the Passover came.
That night the Pharaoh's heart was changed.
He sent for Moses and he said,
"Take your Hebrews out of my country!"
      Moses led the people out of Egypt.
At last they were free, as the Lord had promised.

EXODUS 5-12

25

CROSSING THE RED SEA

The Hebrews camped by the Red Sea.
In the night they heard horses coming.
It was the Egyptians.
The Pharaoh wanted the Hebrews back.
    The Hebrews said to Moses,
"What shall we do?
We have no boats to cross the sea.
But we cannot stay here.
The Egyptians will kill us."
    Then the Lord said to Moses,
"Hold your rod over the sea."
    Moses did as the Lord had said,
and a strong wind blew the sea back.
The water made two walls.
Between them there was a dry path.
The people walked on this to the other side.
    The Egyptian leader cried, "Go after them!"
The Egyptians rode between the walls of water.
    But the Lord said to Moses,
"Put your hand over the water again."
    Moses obeyed, and the waters closed.
They covered the Egyptians and their horses.
    Again the Lord had saved his people.

EXODUS 14

GOD FEEDS HIS PEOPLE

Moses and the Hebrews marched on
into hot, dry, barren country.
They could not find food in the desert.
    The people cried out to Moses,
"We are hungry! We shall die!"
    The next day flakes covered the ground.
They looked like snow.
    "What is it?" the people asked Moses.
    "It is manna," he told them.
"The Lord has given it to you for bread."
    Every morning the manna was there.
The Hebrews ate it and were filled.
    Soon they marched into another desert.
There they could find no water.
    Again the people went to Moses.
"Give us water!" they cried.
    The Lord said to Moses, "Take your rod.
Strike the rock at Horeb."
    With his rod Moses struck the rock.
And water poured from it.
    The people drank the water.
And they praised the Lord.

EXODUS 16, 17

THE TEN COMMANDMENTS

Moses led the Hebrews to Sinai.
And they put up their tents near a mountain.
    The Lord called to Moses from Mount Sinai,
"Come up to me on this mountain."
    The Lord spoke in a loud voice like thunder.
On the mountain He said to Moses,
"These are my commandments,
    Do not adore any God but me.
    Do not bow down to gods of silver or gold.
    Say my name with respect.
    Rest on the Sabbath day, for it is holy.
    Obey your father and your mother.
    Be kind to others and do not hurt them.
    Be faithful to your wife or your husband.
    Do not steal things.
    Always tell the truth.
    Do not wish for things that belong to others."
The Lord wrote his commandments on two stones.
"Give these to my people," said the Lord.

EXODUS 19, 20

THE CALF OF GOLD

Moses stayed on the mountain a long time.
The people asked Aaron, "Where is Moses?
We need him to help us.
He led us out of Egypt.
Make us a god that will help us."
Aaron said, "Give me your gold earrings."
And he used them to make a calf of gold.
The people cried, "This calf is our god."
They did a merry dance before it.
Just then Moses came down the mountain.
He had the commandents in his hands.
"What are the people doing?" he cried.
"Why do they dance before this calf of gold?"
He was very angry.
He threw down the pieces of stone.
They broke into many pieces.
Then he smashed the calf of gold.
Sadly, Moses went up the mountain again.
The Lord said to him,
"Write down my commandents once more."
Moses did as the Lord said.
Then he went down from the mountain.
He gave the people the Lord's commandments.
And they tried to obey them.

EXODUS 32-34

JOSHUA AND THE WALLS OF JERICHO

Moses died after a very long life.
And the Lord set Joshua over the Hebrews.

"Lead my people," the Lord told Joshua.
"Take them into the land I promised them."

But the city of Jericho stood in their way.
Around this city there was a thick wall.
No one went into that city.
No one came out.

"I shall give Jericho into your hands,"
the Lord said to Joshua.
"This is what you must do.
March your men around the city once each day.
Let the priests go with them, blowing horns.
Do this for six days."

"I shall do that, Lord," said Joshua.

Then the Lord told him,
"On the seventh day march around Jericho again.
But do it seven times that day.
The priests will blow their horns each time.
The seventh time they must blow a long blast.
Then the people must shout."

On six days Joshua led his men to the wall.
Each day they marched around the city.

On the seventh day they circled it six times.
The seventh time the priests blew a long blast.

"Shout!" cried Joshua.
"The Lord has given you the city."

The people shouted a great shout.
At once the walls of Jericho fell.
The Hebrews rushed into the city.
Jericho was theirs, as the Lord had said.

JOSHUA 6

33

RUTH AND NAOMI

Naomi, a Hebrew woman, lived in Moab.
Her sons married two women of that country.
Their names were Orpah and Ruth.

In time Naomi's husband and sons died.
"I shall go home to Bethlehem," said Naomi.
She kissed Orpah good-bye.

But Ruth said to Naomi,
"Where you go I shall go.
Your people will be my people.
And your God will be my God."

The two women went to live in Bethlehem.
But life was hard, for they were very poor.
Often they were hungry.

"I shall get food for you," Ruth told Naomi.

The next day Ruth went to a field
that belonged to Boaz, a rich man.
There she picked up grain the workers left behind.

Boaz saw Ruth and he asked a servant,
"Who is that young woman?"

The servant said, "She is Ruth from Moab.
She is picking up grain to make bread for Naomi."

That night Boaz gave Ruth a bag of grain.
"Why are you so kind?" Ruth asked.

"Because you are kind to Naomi," Boaz said.

At home Ruth gave Naomi the grain.
"Boaz gave it to me," she explained.

"Boaz is in our family!" Naomi cried.

In time Ruth married Boaz.
One of their sons was the grandfather
of David, a great king in Israel.

RUTH 1-4

THE KING-TO-BE

The people of Israel wanted a king.
And the Lord said to the prophet Samuel,
"Give them Saul to be their leader."

At first Saul ruled the country well.
But in time he became very wicked.

Then the Lord said to Samuel,
"My people must have a better leader.
Go to Jesse in Bethlehem.
One of his sons will be the next king.
You will know him when you see him."

Jesse showed Samuel his sons.
They were seven fine young men.

Samuel looked at each one.
And each time he shook his head.
Not one of them was the next king.

Then Samuel said to Jesse,
"Are all your sons here?"

Jesse answered, "No. My youngest son,
David, is minding my sheep."

"Bring him to me," said Samuel.

When Samuel saw David he thought,
"This is the boy the Lord wants.
He will be the next king."

From then on the Lord was with David.
But Saul was still king in Israel.

I SAMUEL 8, 9, 15, 16

35

DAVID AND GOLIATH

King Saul's people were in danger.
The Philistines were trying to take their land.
But Saul led his soldiers against their enemy.

Now David's brothers were in the fighting.
His father worried about those fine sons.
Then one day he said to David,
"Take bread to your brothers in camp."

David soon found the Hebrew army on a hill.
Across from it he could see the Philistines.

Suddenly a shout rose from the enemy camp.
Every Hebrew eye turned toward the noise.
It was coming from a very tall man.

Now many Philistines were big.
But this man, Goliath, was over eight feet tall.

Goliath was roaring at the Hebrews.
"Send one of your soldiers to fight me."

But David cried, "Who is this man?
How dare he shout at the Lord's soldiers!
I will fight him."

King Saul heard this and he said,
"David, you cannot fight this giant!
You are only a boy."

"The Lord will take care of me," said David.
He picked up five stones from a brook.
These he put into his bag.
He carried a sling in his hand.
Then he went out to face Goliath.
Goliath saw him coming and laughed.
But David cried, "I come in the Lord's name.
He will give you into my hands."
Goliath went forward to meet the Hebrew.
Then David took a stone from his bag.
He fitted it into his sling and he threw it.
The stone hit Goliath right above the eyes.
Down went the giant, flat on the ground.
The Philistines cried, "Goliath is dead!"
They turned and ran, every one of them.
The Hebrews shouted for joy.
David had saved the day for his people.

I SAMUEL 17

SAUL AND DAVID

The Hebrews sang songs in praise of David.
"He killed the giant Goliath," they said.

"Why don't they praise me?" asked King Saul.
"I am their king."

He turned to his son Jonathan.
"You must kill this David," he said.

But Jonathan and David were good friends.
Jonathan hurried to David and warned him,
"Be careful. My father wants to kill you."

David ran away and hid in a deep cave.

One day King Saul went there to rest.
But the cave was very dark.
And the king thought he was alone.

On soft feet David crept up behind him.
He cut off a piece of the king's robe.

Soon after, the king left the cave.
But David ran after him and cried, "My Lord!
Today God gave you into my hands.
But I did not hurt you.
See! I cut this piece from your robe."

The king said, "I wanted to kill you.
But you have done only good to me.
May the Lord bless you."

In time Saul died.
And David became king of Israel.

I SAMUEL 18-20, 24-31
II SAMUEL 1-5

ELIJAH AND KING AHAB

Years after David, Israel was ruled by Ahab.
He was a very wicked king.

The Lord saw this and He was not pleased.
His holy man, Elijah, went to the king and said,
"You do not obey God's law.
The Lord will punish you for being wicked.
No rain will fall in Israel for many years."

It happened just as Elijah had said.
Day after day no rain fell.
No grain grew in the dry fields.
No fruit grew on the trees.

Ahab became very angry at Elijah.
And the Lord said to Elijah,
"Go and hide by the brook Cherith.
My ravens will bring you food."

Elijah obeyed the Lord.
He lived by the brook and he drank its water.
The ravens brought him food every morning.
They brought him bread and meat every evening.

But still no rain fell in the land.

1 KINGS 16, 17

THE WIDOW'S SON

The brook Cherith dried up,
and Elijah had no more water.

He said to a poor woman,
"Please give me water and bread."

The woman brought him water in a cup.
"I have but a handful of grain," she told him.
"But I will give you what I have."

"You are a good woman," said Elijah.
"I promise that you will always have food.
You will have it until the rain falls again."

From that time on she always had food.

But one day she came to him and said,
"What have you done to me, man of God?
Look! My child is dead!"

Elijah took the dead child.
He laid him on his own bed.

"O Lord God!" cried Elijah.
"This woman was kind to me.
Please give life to her little child."

The Lord heard Elijah's prayer.
The little boy came back to life.

The happy woman thanked him.
"You are indeed a man of God," she said.
And she took her little boy home.

I KINGS 17

41

ELISHA AND THE POOR WOMAN

Elisha was a holy man in Israel.
One day a woman came to him and said,
"My husband is dead and I have no money.
But I owe money to all my friends.
How can I pay it back?
How can I get money to feed my sons?"
Elisha asked, "Do you have food at home?"
"I have only a jar of oil," she said.
Elisha told her, "Go to your friends.
Ask them to lend you jars and pots and bowls."
The woman did this.
Then Elisha told her,
"Pour oil from your jar into the first bowl.
Then pour more into the second bowl."
But the woman said, "Sir!
The oil in my jar cannot fill one bowl.
How can I fill two bowls from it?"
Elisha said to her, "Do as I say."
And so the woman kept pouring.
Soon every jar and pot and bowl was filled.
So she asked Elisha, "What shall I do now?"
He said to her, "Sell the oil.
You will get money to pay what you owe.
Then you will have lots of money left.
It will buy food for you and your sons."
And that is what happened.

II KINGS 4

THE STRANGE WORDS ON THE WALL

Three hundred years passed after Elisha lived.
In those years Israel had suffered many troubles.

One trouble was Babylon's war with the Hebrews.
The king of Babylon went into Jerusalem.
He stole gold vessels from the Lord's Temple.
He brought Hebrews from Jerusalem to Babylon.
One of them was Daniel, a wise young man.

In time another king became ruler of Babylon.
One night this king had a dinner.
His friends came and ate from gold vessels.

Suddenly the king rose and pointed at the wall.
There a hand was writing strange words.

"What do the words mean?" the king cried.

No one could tell him.

Then the king sent for Daniel, the Hebrew.

Daniel said, "The Lord is not pleased with you.
You are eating from His Temple's gold vessels."

But the king said, "Never mind that.
Tell me the meaning of the words."

"Here is what they mean," Daniel answered.
"Your kingdom will be taken from you.
It will be broken up and given to another ruler."

That very night the king was killed.
His kingdom was given to Darius, king of the Medes.

DANIEL 1, 5

DANIEL IN THE LIONS' DEN

Darius was king of a very large country.
And he named three men to help him rule it.
Daniel, the Hebrew, was one of these men.

Daniel ruled his part of the country well.
The king saw this and he said,
"I shall put Daniel over the other two rulers."

The two rulers heard the king's words.
"We must not let this happen," they said.
And they thought of a way to hurt Daniel.
They would trick him into breaking a law.

They went to King Darius and said,
"O king! Please make a new law.
Say that people may worship no one but you.
Let no one break this law.
The one who does will be thrown to the lions."

The king signed this foolish law.

The next day Daniel went to his room.
He got down on his knees and prayed to God.

But the two rulers were hiding nearby.
They heard him praying.

At once they went to Darius and said,
"O king! Daniel is breaking your law.
He is worshiping the Hebrews' God.
You must throw him to the lions."

"No, I will not!" said the king.

But the rulers said, "He broke your law.
Not even you, O king, can change that law."

And so Daniel was thrown to the lions.
All that night the king worried about him.
In the morning he went to the lions' den.
He cried, "Daniel, has your God saved you?"

And Daniel called back, "Yes, O king!
God has kept the lions from hurting me."

The king was happy that Daniel was alive.
And he praised the God of Daniel.

DANIEL 6

Perhaps Daniel taught the king an old song of praise.
It is a song the Hebrews had sung for many, many years:
"It is good to praise the Lord.
Praise him, all you shining stars!
Praise him, sun and moon!
Praise the Lord, angels on high!
Praise him, mountains and hills!
Praise him, old men and children, too!
Let everyone praise the name of the Lord."

PSALMS 148

45